A Celebration of Friendship

A Celebration of Friendship

*A Keepsake Devotional Featuring the
Inspirational Poetry of Helen Steiner Rice*

BARBOUR
PUBLISHING

ISBN 978-1-60260-715-6

Devotional writing provided by Rebecca Currington in association with Snapdragon Group.ᔆᴹ

The poetry of Helen Steiner Rice is published under a licensing agreement with the Helen Steiner Rice Foundation Fund, LLC.

Cover and interior illustration: Todd Williams

Published by Barbour Publishing, Inc., P.O. Box 719, Uhrichsville, Ohio 44683
www.barbourbooks.com

Our mission is to publish and distribute inspirational products offering exceptional value and biblical encouragement to the masses.

Member of the
Evangelical Christian
Publishers Association

Printed in China.

Contents

INTRODUCTION

*W*ho could imagine that our great and mighty God who created the entire universe would ever be interested in a simple concept like friendship? But He is! He has extended His hand of friendship to us and made it clear that He desires us to extend a hand of friendship to each other in return. His friendship is both a gift and a command—one we are privileged to accept and obey.

Friendship can be hard work at times, but it is a sign of God's presence in our lives. Friends teach us patience, tolerance, forgiveness, courage, and tenacity. They challenge us, inspire us, comfort us, affirm us, and hold our hands in tough times. They try hard to protect our feelings and yet are often the only ones who will tell us the truth. God uses our friends to help Him shape and mold us into the people He created us to be.

As you read through the pages of this book, we hope you will be inspired by the artistry and wisdom of the gifted poet Helen Steiner Rice. We have coupled each one of her beautiful poems with a devotional that we pray will draw you closer in friendship to our amazing God and the other friends He has placed in your life.

God bless you as we celebrate friendship together.

What Is Love?

*W*hat is love? No words can define it—
It's something so great only God could design it.
Wonder of wonders, beyond man's conception—
And only in God can love find true perfection...

For love means much more than small words can express,
For what man calls love is so very much less
Than the beauty and depth and the true richness of
God's gift to mankind of compassion from above.

For love has become a word that's misused,
Perverted, distorted, and often abused,
To speak of light romance or some affinity for,
A passing attraction that is seldom much more

Than a mere interlude of inflamed fascination,
A romantic fling of no lasting duration. . .
But love is enduring and patient and kind—
It judges all with the heart, not the mind. . .

And love can transform the most commonplace
Into beauty and splendor and sweetness and grace. . .
For love is unselfish, giving more than it takes—
And no matter what happens, love never forsakes.

It's faithful and trusting and always believing,
Guileless and honest and never deceiving.
Yes, love is beyond what man can define,
For love is immortal and God's gift is divine!

~HSR

Friendship Is Love

Friends Are Life's Gift of Love

*I*f people like me didn't know people like you,
Life would lose its meaning and its richness, too. . .
For the friends that we make are life's gift of love,
And I think friends are sent right from heaven above. . .
And thinking of you somehow makes me feel
That God is love and He's very real.

~ *HSR*

FACES IN THE CROWD

These God-chosen lives all around—what splendid friends they make!
PSALM 16:3 MSG

Have you ever stopped to imagine how many people cross your path in the course of a year? Not just the ones you recognize or even the ones you notice, but *all* the people you encounter? The young mother who passes you in the supermarket aisle with her two little ones in tow. Or the woman sitting in the next chair at the hair salon, casting a timid smile your way. How about the man who delivers your mail or fixes your car or briefly passes you on the street? The number is probably astronomical. Most of these chance encounters are easily forgotten within a few moments—if remembered at all.

But now and then you look up and see instant recognition in the eyes of a stranger. Soon that stranger becomes a friend. What makes that person stand out from the teeming sea of people you pass by each day? The answer could well be the hand of God.

Our God is a friendly God: kind, loving, and generous. He's always there for us when we need Him. He is the personification of friendship. Is it so hard to believe, then, that God takes time to point out those special faces in the crowd to us? That He chooses our friends for us?

Begin to think of your friends as an expression of God's love for you—His remarkable gifts—because that's exactly what they are!

A Gift of Love

Time is not measured by the years that you live
But by the deeds that you do and the joy that you give...
And from birthday to birthday, the good Lord above
Bestows on His children the gift of His love,
Asking us only to share it with others
By treating all people not as strangers but brothers...
And each day, as it comes, brings a new chance to each one
To live to the fullest, leaving nothing undone
That would brighten the life or lighten the load
Of some weary traveler lost on life's road...
So what does it matter how long we may live
If as long as we live, we unselfishly give.

~ HSR

Time Flies

There is a time for everything, and a season for every activity under heaven.
ECCLESIASTES 3:1

Time flies—really, it does. One day summer is ending, and then we glance at the calendar again and realize it's almost Christmas. The New Year barely passes before warm winds melt the remnants of winter and push us once again into the dog days of summer. Where does the time go?

If this seems like your life, you are not entirely to blame. Our culture moves at a frightening pace, placing extraordinary demands on us. We are expected to be good mothers, wives, husbands, fathers, sisters, and brothers; make room for careers; eat right; get proper exercise; and keep our homes well maintained. If we have children, our schedules become even more demanding—full of soccer games, dance lessons, birthday parties, dental appointments, and late-night schoolwork. Unfortunately, the first thing that gets lost in all that activity is friendship. We simply can't find time to get together, to keep up, or to be there for one another.

If we are to have friends in this life, we must consciously make that call, put that name on our schedule, and insist on stopping for just a while to listen—to share with another person our thoughts and affection.

If you're struggling to nurture your many relationships, be sure to ask God to help you make time for the friends He has given you. Maybe that just means one phone call a week or lunch once a month—whatever it takes to maintain a meaningful connection. Your life will be much richer for it.

It's a Wonderful World

In spite of the fact we complain and lament
And view this old world with much discontent,
Deploring conditions and grumbling because
There's so much injustice and so many flaws,
It's a wonderful world, and it's people like you
Who make it that way by the things that they do.
For a warm, ready smile or a kind, thoughtful deed
Or a hand outstretched in an hour of need
Can change our whole outlook and make the world bright
Where a minute before just nothing seemed right.
It's a wonderful world, and it always will be
If we keep our eyes open and focused to see
The wonderful things we are capable of
When we open our hearts to God and His love.

~ HSR

PEOPLE FIRST

Some friends play at friendship but a true friend sticks closer than one's nearest kin.
PROVERBS 18:24 NRSV

The Bible says that God created us in His image and intended for us to follow His example. And the first thing we learn about this God, whom we are supposed to model our lives after, is that He puts people first. He walked and talked with Adam and Eve in the Garden of Eden. He called Moses and Abraham His friends. He could have sat on His throne and watched us from a distance. Instead, He became one of us, a human man, and gave us a living example of how we should arrange our priorities.

Jesus' mission was greater than any before or since. His was important work—so important that nothing could ever match it. And yet He chose twelve friends to share the most intimate details of His life with. He engaged them in conversation, ate with them, and walked the countryside with them. He also found time to regularly visit His distant acquaintances and enjoy their hospitality. His friends always came first.

Putting people first is the definition of love. Making that first gesture of friendship—being the first one to pick up the phone and ask how someone's doing or clearing your schedule to have lunch with a friend who's going through a hard time— that is love, pure and simple.

When it comes to friendship, the smallest things mean a lot. Follow God's example and reach out in love, making your friends a top priority.

A Pattern for Living

"*L*ove one another as I have loved you"
May seem impossible to do,
But if you will try to trust and believe,
Great are the joys that you will receive.
For love makes us patient, understanding, and kind,
And we judge with our hearts and not with our minds.
For as soon as love enters the heart's open door,
The faults we once saw are not there anymore,
And the things that seem wrong begin to look right
When viewed in the softness of love's gentle light.
For love works in ways that are wondrous and strange,
And there is nothing in life that love cannot change,
And all that God promised will someday come true
When you love one another the way He loved you.

~*HSR*

LOVE COVERS

Bear with each other and forgive whatever grievances you may have against one another. Forgive as the Lord forgave you.
COLOSSIANS 3:13

*T*here's a big drawback to spending time with people, even if they are your best friends in the world. You know what it is? Easy—they're people! And people are flawed.

We were all created in God's image, and we are still like Him. But the free will God granted us got us into trouble. Sin and selfishness entered our lives and stole our perfection. Of course, God did not abandon us in our imperfect state. He made a way of salvation and brought us back into His family. But in this life, we are still dealing with our flaws—and lots of them—in ourselves and in the people around us.

The wonder of God's love is that when we turned our selfish hearts away from Him, He considered regaining a relationship with us more important than punishing our offenses. He went to incomprehensible lengths to close the gap between us and Him. The lesson He left behind is that we must be willing to do the same for the people we love.

Perhaps there is a friend in your life who frequently offends: not the hard-hearted person who doesn't care about others at all, but someone who is truly a friend and has just tripped over their humanness. Perhaps you are that person in someone else's life. Let love cover the hurt and disappointment. Go out of your way to make amends just as your heavenly Father did. That's the way of love.

REMEMBER THIS

Great is the power of might and mind,
But only love can make us kind,
And all we are or hope to be
Is empty pride and vanity.
If love is not a part of all,
The greatest man is very small.

~ HSR

What Life Is All About

Forgive as the Lord forgave you. And over all these virtues put on love,
which binds them all together in perfect unity.
Colossians 3:13–14

*L*ove rules! It is the power by which God commands the universe. It is the golden cord that holds all things together. When we walk in love, we act accordingly and become extensions of the Great Creator—His messengers of kindness. It's an awesome responsibility, but it is also an amazing privilege.

Loving and being loved is what life is all about. It reaches to the core of who we were created to be, and friends are a delightful part of that reality. Can you remember a time when a simple hug from a friend left you feeling stronger and more confident? Have you ever had a friend stop by or give you a call when you were feeling down? Most likely that visit or phone call made you feel better. Friends can change the tone of your day just by listening and laughing. Friendship is powerful because it is fueled by the power of love.

True friendship can't be faked, at least not for long. We are fooled only when our own motives become self-centered or insincere. When we find a true friend, we look past the facade to the real person inside. We do as God does—we look at the heart.

Friendship is a responsibility and a privilege. Cherish every moment you spend with true friends and thank God often for bringing them into your life. Love them deeply and sincerely. Overlook their faults and imperfections. And remember, you are richly blessed.

Friendship Is Kindness

His Footsteps

When someone does a kindness,
It always seems to me
That's the way God up in heaven
Would like us all to be.
For when we bring some pleasure
To another human heart,
We have followed in His footsteps
And we've had a little part
In serving God who loves us.
For I'm very sure it's true
That in serving those around us,
We serve and please God, too.

~ HSR

Conscious Acts of Kindness

"Do what is right and true. Be kind and merciful to each other."
Zechariah 7:9 ncv

*K*indness doesn't happen by accident. It is a conscious action, and that's what makes it so special. Think of it this way: The sun doesn't come up each morning as an act of kindness to human beings. God created it and set it in motion on a specific path. It simply does what it was created to do—provide light and heat to the solar system. But human beings have the gift of conscious intent. We can choose to do a thing and then carry it out. That makes us uniquely capable of initiating kind acts and speaking kind words.

Kindness is essential to friendship. When someone does something for us—something unexpected and unearned—it tells us that we are not alone on the road of life. What a sweet relief that is! Then as kindnesses are exchanged, we begin to understand that we were meant to be there for each other, and friendship ultimately blossoms.

You were meant to be kind, but unlike the sun, you have been given the gift to choose your own course. That smile, those kind words, the favor someone needs—none of that will happen unless you decide to make it happen. You have the ability to bless others and simultaneously bless yourself as a result.

Spend some time today considering ways to initiate kindness. Lighten someone's burden, cheer someone's day, or lend a hand. Then stand back and watch friendship grow.

The World Would Be a Nicer Place If We Traveled at a Slower Pace

*A*mid stresses and strain, much too many to mention,
And pressure-packed days filled with turmoil and tension,
We seldom have time to be friendly or kind,
For we're harassed and hurried and always behind. . .
And while we've more gadgets and buttons to press,
Making leisure time greater and laboring less,
And our standards of living they claim have improved
And repressed inhibitions have been freed and removed,
It seems all this progress and growth is for naught,
For daily we see a world more distraught. . .
So what does it matter if man reaches his goal
And gains the whole world but loses his soul?
For what have we won if in gaining this end
We've been much too busy to be kind to a friend?
And what is there left to make the heart sing
When life is a cold and mechanical thing?
And are we but puppets of controlled automation
Instead of joint heirs to God's gift of creation?

~*HSR*

In the Moment

Don't forget your friend.
PROVERBS 27:10 NCV

Have you ever run into an old friend at a restaurant, in a parking lot, or even at church and said, "Oh my goodness, it's been too long since we've seen each other. We need to catch up. Let's get together soon!" Right there in that moment, you remember what you meant to each other, and feelings of warm affection surface. You really do want to regain the joy of that friendship, but as soon as you walk away, life floods back in on you. Out of sight is once again out of mind.

If this has happened to you, you're not alone. It has happened to almost everyone. What a price we pay for our frenzied lifestyles and overwhelming schedules. In our effort to live full and successful lives, we forget that friendship is a gift from God, intended to give us greater enjoyment of the lives we lead while providing us with other essentials like encouragement, insight, and sound advice.

The next time this happens to you, take it as a message from God to slow down and enjoy the blessings He has placed in your life. Ask your friend right there on the spot how best to make contact and then agree on a specific time to do so.

God doesn't want to change your life entirely. He's proud of the things you accomplish. He just wants you to enjoy the blessings He has given you along the way, especially the blessing of friendship.

The Richness in Kindness

It's not fortune or fame or worldwide acclaim
That makes for true greatness; you'll find
It's the wonderful art of teaching the heart
To always be thoughtful and kind!

~ HSR

Kindness Is a God Thing

You know that the Lord will reward everyone for whatever good he does.
Ephesians 6:8

If you've read the Bible's account of Jesus' life, you probably noticed that He was a supremely kind man. He heard the cry of the blind man and restored his sight. He had compassion for the lepers and healed them. He listened to the common people, those who had no power, and He helped them. They recognized the kindness in His eyes and swarmed around Him, looking for even so much as a touch. He spent an evening with a hated tax collector who had climbed a tree just to get a peek at the Teacher from Galilee. On several occasions, Jesus fed thousands of hungry and tired people.

Jesus was kind to strangers, particularly those in need. But He was even kinder to those He loved in a special way—His friends. He took time out of His day for them, ate with them, encouraged them, and taught them. He even raised one of them from the dead.

Kindness is a God thing, and that's something He is longing to instill in each of us. Ask God to open your heart and teach you His ways of compassion. Keep your eyes and ears open for those precious assignments. They won't all seem like a big deal. Something as small as a sincere hug can make a big impact on someone who feels lonely or forgotten. You don't know the hearts of those around you, but God does and He will guide you. And as He does, you will become more like Him.

FLOWERS LEAVE THEIR FRAGRANCE
ON THE HAND THAT BESTOWS THEM

There's an old Chinese proverb that if practiced each day
Would change the whole world in a wonderful way.
Its truth is so simple, it's easy to do,
And it works every time and successfully, too.
For you can't do a kindness without a reward,
Not in silver or gold but in joy from the Lord.
You can't light a candle to show others the way
Without feeling the warmth of that bright little ray,
And you can't pluck a rose all fragrant with dew
Without part of its fragrance remaining with you.

~ HSR

SOMETHING TO REMEMBER

As we have opportunity, let us do good to all people,
especially to those who belong to the family of believers.
GALATIANS 6:10

Kindness doesn't have to be a solo act. In many cases in the New Testament, Jesus carried out acts of kindness with the help of His friends, especially the twelve who traveled with Him as He taught and ministered to the masses. They distributed the food when He fed five thousand from a small boy's sack lunch. They were there praying beside Him when He healed the sick. Kindness is not just something you do *for* your friends; it's something you do *with* your friends—and the opportunities are endless.

Take a good look around you and then call your friends. See who would be able to go with you to visit a nursing home, organize a blood drive, or help someone move. How about organizing a cookie drive for the troops or providing relief for an overwhelmed mother? What about pitching in to do yard work for a neighbor who has been sick, repairing someone's car, or keeping your ears open for job leads to share with displaced workers at your church?

These joint ventures of kindness will bring you closer together, and they will provide experiences that you and your friends will never forget. Goodness always blesses us as we go.

Choose a day and a task and make those phone calls. Your friends might be slow to respond at first, but once they realize the joy that comes from kindness, they won't want to miss a thing.

Take Time to Be Kind

*K*indness is a virtue given by the Lord;
It pays dividends in happiness and joy is its reward.
For if you practice kindness in all you say and do,
The Lord will wrap His kindness around your heart
    and you.

~ *HSR*

A True Friend

"Give to the one who asks you, and do not turn away from the one who wants to borrow from you."

Matthew 5:42

Genuine kindness given and received in love is the greatest bond of friendship. Why else would you do all you do for your friends, and why would they do all they do for you? When you need a ride or help getting ready for a party, who do you call? When you need help moving a couch or getting your boat ready for fishing season, who do you call? Friends are always on call for kindnesses like picking up the mail when you're out of town or "the big three" (dog sitting, house sitting, and babysitting). Who else would you trust with those responsibilities but a true friend?

Learning to give and receive kindness may be one of the most important aspects of friendship because it helps us to genuinely develop the Christlike virtues of selflessness and compassion. It draws our focus away from ourselves and onto the needs of others. We become more like our heavenly Father by learning to put people first.

The mutual kindness that friendship provides can be great fun as well. Who knew that helping a friend put up new wallpaper could make you laugh so long and hard? Kindness is a pursuit that pays great personal rewards. And that's not all! It also gives God a reason to pour out His blessings on the both of you. What a deal!

Reward

If you carve your name in a man's heart
With a kindly word and a laugh,
You can be mighty sure that your tombstone
Will be carved with the right epitaph.

~ HSR

BEING A FRIEND

Those who love a pure heart and are gracious in speech will have the king as a friend.
PROVERBS 22:11 NRSV

*T*hose people in your life, the ones you would label as "kind"
or "sweet" or "loving," who are they? Logically, you might think
those would be the people who have done huge favors for
you—kindnesses that are over the moon, so to speak. But think
about it a little longer, and you'll probably realize that those
people you think of as kind, sweet, and loving are the ones who
always greet you with a smile and an encouraging word. They
surprise you with an unexpected compliment or lighten your
day by making you laugh.

You can be one of those people everyone loves, everyone
wants to spend time with. Anyone can. It's all about taking
the focus off yourself and putting it on the other person. The
great Dale Carnegie said, "You can make more friends in two
months by becoming interested in other people than you can in
two years by trying to get other people interested in you."

If you are in the mood to make new friends, ask God to
help you really "see" each person who comes across your path.
Be that kind, sweet, and loving person who takes time to listen
and always lights up with a big smile. Be that someone who
makes others feel special! Your looks won't matter. Your bank
account won't either. Nor will anyone care how smart you are.
You'll be surrounded by friends because you're you.

On Life's Busy Thoroughfares, We Meet with Angels Unawares

*T*he unexpected kindness from an unexpected place,
A hand outstretched in friendship, a smile on someone's face,
A word of understanding spoken in a time of trial
Are unexpected miracles that make life more worthwhile.
We know not how it happened that in an hour of need
Somebody out of nowhere proved to be a friend indeed. . .
For God has many messengers we fail to recognize,
But He sends them when we need them,
    and His ways are wondrous and wise. . .
So keep looking for an angel and keep listening to hear,
For on life's busy, crowded streets,
    you will find God's presence near.

~*JHSR*

God's Work

Give freely and spontaneously. Don't have a stingy heart. The way you handle matters like this triggers GOD, your God's, blessing in everything you do, all your work and ventures.
DEUTERONOMY 15:10 MSG

We all love surprises. A friend comes by with brownies—just because! A neighbor mows his yard and yours, too, just to be nice. Surprises are great. But imagine for a moment that you are poverty-stricken and someone, a stranger, surprises you with a gift that you really need out of the kindness of their heart. Maybe it's just a few dollars or a sack lunch, but wouldn't it mean so much more? When you are lost in a sea of poverty, every little bit matters and kindness is never taken for granted. What if someone offered you a coat or a pair of boots? Wouldn't you see that person as a messenger of God?

When we are kind to the poor and needy, we become God's messengers, sent to lessen human suffering by demonstrating His great mercy and compassion. We become His hands and feet, reaching out to the powerless and forgotten. Because we do not forget them, we show that God has not forgotten them. Helping those who cannot help themselves is truly God's work.

Ask God to make you a friend of those in need, giving them first and foremost the dignity and respect they deserve as God's children. Then look for opportunities to help, not only through charities but also one-on-one, reaching out to the homeless man you pass each morning or the family two blocks down whose home was destroyed by fire. Show God's love by being a friend to the friendless. In this way, we become the friends of God.

THE BEAUTY OF SPRING

God lives in the beauty that comes with spring—
The colorful flowers, the birds that sing—
And He lives in people as kind as you,
And He lives in all the nice things you do.

~HSR

The Garden Within

If we love one another, God lives in us and his love is made complete in us.
1 JOHN 4:12

O ne of the cornerstones of the Christian faith is that God sent His Son to live among us as a human being, to die in our place to pay the debt of our sin, and to rise from the grave, conquering death once and for all. Not only did He complete His mission perfectly in every way, but He also left His Holy Spirit here to dwell in us. We live with the Spirit of our holy Savior illuminating us from the inside out. Words simply cannot express the amazing nature of this precious gift.

If we let Him, He orchestrates our lives from within, giving us the desire to reach out with kindness to others, to befriend the friendless, to live lives of honor and truth. Like the flowers of spring, He causes beauty to spring forth in our lives from within. The warmth of His love for us melts our cold hearts and draws out our inner goodness.

Perhaps you find it difficult to reach out to others. You may be shy in nature or uncertain and lacking confidence. Fortunately, you do not have to depend only on yourself. God is there to help you pass along His goodness to others. Ask Him to open your eyes to the beauty and generosity He has planted within you. Then give Him permission to show it off to the world through your kind words and generous deeds.

The Garden of Friendship

*T*here is no garden
So complete
But roses could make
The place more sweet.
There is no life
So rich and rare
But one more friend
Could enter there.
Like roses in a garden,
Kindness fills the air
With a certain bit of sweetness
As it touches everywhere.

~ *HSR*

FRIENDS ARE LIKE FLOWERS

Friends love through all kinds of weather.
PROVERBS 17:17 MSG

*I*n God's eyes you can never have too much kindness or too many friends decorating your life. There is always room for one more flower in your garden. After all, each one has its own style and beauty. Close your eyes and imagine this:

In the center of your friendship garden are the tulips—your closest friends, those whom you've entrusted with your thoughts and dreams, those you can trust with your confidences. Even when they aren't lifting their soft, colorful heads to the sky, they are always there, just below the surface. They are capable of withstanding the heat of summer and the cold of winter and still spring forth without fail whenever you need them. Behind the tulips are the roses. These friends require much care, and their thorns can leave you feeling wounded at times, but they bring a beautiful fragrance to your life.

To the side are the daisies. These are the friends you don't see often, but when you do, joy and laughter fill the air. When you're feeling blue and things aren't going your way, it's wonderful to see a daisy friend coming up the front walk. On the other side are the tiger lilies, those friends who are always challenging you to grow into the person God created you to be. We all need a few tiger lilies in our gardens.

There are many kinds of friends planted in the garden of your heart. Take a long look around and then water them with your tears of thankfulness.

Friendship Is Sharing

THE BLESSINGS OF SHARING

*O*nly what we give away
Enriches us from day to day,
For not in getting but in giving
Is found the lasting joy of living.
For no one ever had a part
In sharing treasures of the heart
Who did not feel the impact of
The magic mystery of God's love.
Love alone can make us kind
And give us joy and peace of mind,
So live with joy unselfishly
And you'll be blessed abundantly.

~ *HSR*

JUST LIKE JESUS

Now may our Lord Jesus Christ himself and God our Father,
who loved us and by his grace gave us eternal comfort and a wonderful hope,
comfort you and strengthen you in every good thing you do and say.
2 THESSALONIANS 2:16–17 NLT

If kindness is the essence of friendship, sharing is its central activity. Friends share everything—their joys and sorrows, their dreams and disappointments, their goals and obstacles. They often share hobbies and interests. Yes, the best of friends share the best and the worst of everything. Have you ever shared a sunburn with a friend after spending a day at the beach together? Have you shared the frustration of a joint project gone wrong? Have you ever borrowed a friend's prized possession, or loaned a friend yours?

Sharing is the model God has given us for friendship through His own words and actions. He became a human being so that He could see life from our perspective. He wanted to share the human experience with us. Now He is able to be the ultimate friend because He truly knows what we go through. His actions show us the cost of friendship.

It's easy to share only those things that are comfortable, but if you want to be a true friend—the kind of friend God is to us—you must be willing to share the good and the bad. You must be willing to walk with your friend even when that means traversing the lowest valleys life has to offer. But don't be discouraged; you'll also get to take in the mountaintops together, sharing all the beauty of life's joy and gladness.

Giving Is the Key to Living

*E*very day is a reason for giving,
And giving is the key to living. . .
So let us give ourselves away,
Not just today but every day.
And remember, a kind and thoughtful deed,
Or a hand outstretched in a time of need,
Is the rarest of gifts, for it is a part
Not of the purse but of a loving heart. . .
And he who gives of himself will find
True joy of heart and peace of mind.

~ *HSR*

GIVING YOURSELF

It is God who works in you to will and to act according to his good purpose.
PHILIPPIANS 2:13

Sit back, close your eyes, and reminisce. . . . Is there a face
that stands out—someone who extended a hand of friendship
to you? Where were you in your life at that time? Perhaps you
were new at school or you had just moved into the neighbor-
hood. It could be you were attending a particular church for the
first time or just starting a new job. Only you know the specific
details of that first encounter. Almost certainly, though, you
were feeling a bit insecure and out of place. Then that special
person came along and reached out a hand, and you relaxed.
Think for a moment about how much that meant to you.

We rarely realize in this life how much our actions can
mean to others. What might seem like a small gesture of wel-
come could be an unforgettable gift to someone who is taking
their first tentative steps in a new place or phase of life. Fears
can be banished by something as simple as a smile or an invita-
tion to join in.

You don't know how much the gift of sharing yourself
means to others. You might think it is nothing, but for a person
who is longing to see a smiling face, it could be a very big deal
indeed—something that person will always remember.

Now, offer a prayer of thanksgiving for that person who
made a difference in your life.

Give Lavishly!
Live Abundantly!

The more you give, the more you get;
The more you laugh, the less you fret.
The more you do unselfishly,
The more you live abundantly.
The more of everything you share,
The more you'll always have to spare.
The more you love, the more you'll find
That life is good and friends are kind,
For only what we give away
Enriches us from day to day.

~ HSR

Unchangeable Principles

God is able to provide you with every blessing in abundance, so that by always having enough of everything, you may share abundantly in every good work.
2 Corinthians 9:8 NRSV

God loves us and it is His desire to bless us abundantly, without measure. Like any good father, He longs to give His children all manner of wonderful gifts. To benefit from these blessings, however, we must open our lives to some of God's unchangeable principles. Do these apply to your life?

Giving versus withholding. God never intended for the blessings He has placed in our lives to remain only with us. They are meant to be passed from one to another without being diminished in the slightest.

Laughter versus worry. God's blessings and our worry cannot abide together. Letting go of worry and replacing it with joy and thankfulness can be a daunting task, but it's possible if we make a conscious decision to hand over our worries to God and receive His comfort in return.

Selflessness versus selfishness. Selfishness causes us to draw back. It isolates us, like the child who cannot play with his toys because he is too busy keeping them away from the other children. But when we lay down our treasures, our hands are free to receive new and wonderful gifts from God.

Open your heart to give, to laugh, to share. Honor God's principles and your life will be rich with blessings, friends, and the wonders of God's love.

THE WORLD NEEDS FRIENDLY FOLKS LIKE YOU

*I*n this troubled world it's refreshing to find
Someone who still has the time to be kind,
Someone who still has the faith to believe
That the more that you give, the more you receive,
Someone who's ready by thoughts, word, or deed
To reach out a hand in the hour of need.

~ *HSR*

Light and Hope

Be an example to the believers with your words, your actions,
your love, your faith, and your pure life.
1 Timothy 4:12 NCV

We live in a magnificent world, a world that was created without the taint of sadness and tragedy and hardship. These came as a result of sin, and for now, they are the garments our world must wear. One day God will restore the earth to its original glory, and we will know the peace and joy of His original plan. For now, though, He has promised to be ever present with us as we live out our time here. In fact, He has assigned us to bring light and hope to those who can't yet comprehend the bright future in store for us.

When you are kind, when you have no place for bitterness in your life, when your heart is filled to overflowing with optimism and joy, when your thoughts and actions transcend the cold realities we live with daily and attach themselves to the greater reality of God's love and care—that's when we become messengers of hope to this world.

What a great privilege it is to be God's spokespersons for all He has planned for us. What an honor it is to be able to comfort the brokenhearted and lend a hand to those crushed by hardship. We each have been given the strength to extend a hand of friendship to someone who is lonely, tired, and discouraged. Don't miss an opportunity to remind those around you that God has given us a remarkable resource—each other. There is strength in sharing His goodness and love.

Heart Gifts

It's not the things that can be bought
That are life's richest treasures;
It's just the little "heart gifts"
That money cannot measure.
A cheerful smile, a friendly word,
A sympathetic nod
Are priceless little treasures
From the storehouse of our God.
They are the things that can't be bought
With silver or with gold,
For thoughtfulness and kindness
And love are never sold.
They are the priceless things in life
For which no one can pay,
And the giver finds rich recompense
In giving them away.

~ HSR

TRULY PRICELESS

*H*ave you ever stopped to wonder what the world would be like if money and the commercialism it spawns vanished? It isn't that money is evil. We all know it serves a vital purpose. Without it, we would have no practical way to purchase necessary commodities like food, clothing, housing, and transportation. We need money to care for our families and keep them safe and healthy.

The trouble is that money has come to mean everything. It has become not only the currency of our physical needs but also the primary focus of our emotional needs. How would our lives be transformed if we gave each other gifts of kindness and friendship? These gifts cannot be purchased with money—not because they lack value but because they are priceless. And these are the gifts that will be remembered, rather than the items advertisers convince us to buy. We go with the big price tags because we fear being thought of as cheap, but nothing could be further from the truth.

Consider making a deal with your friends that for the upcoming year, your gifts for one another must be of the "priceless" variety (no cash exchanged). Think each gift through until you find just the right expression of your love and devotion for one another. Your love will almost certainly deepen, and you will all learn to value the true gifts in your lives.

THE GIFT OF FRIENDSHIP

Friendship is a priceless gift that cannot be bought or sold,
But its value is far greater than a mountain made of gold—
For gold is cold and lifeless, it can neither see nor hear,
And in the time of trouble, it is powerless to cheer.
It has no ears to listen, no heart to understand;
It cannot bring you comfort or reach out a helping hand—
So when you ask God for a gift, be thankful if He sends
Not diamonds, pearls, or riches, but the love of real true friends.

~ HSR

A Gift of Unspeakable Value

"Why spend money on what is not bread, and your labor on what does not satisfy? Listen, listen to me, and eat what is good, and your soul will delight in the richest of fare."
ISAIAH 55:2

It's human nature to think having a pile of money at our feet would make us happy and solve all our problems. If we could just win the lottery or receive an unexpected inheritance from some distant relative, our worries would be over. We kid ourselves. A quick look around and we would realize that money has nothing to do with happiness—in fact, it can often derail it.

Money serves a purpose in our lives, but the really important things can't be acquired with money. The wealthy, for example, must always be on the lookout for ulterior motives. They don't even have the luxury of accepting the kindness of others at face value. Who would think that such a small thing could mean so much? With all their money, they cannot buy the devotion of a true friend.

The reality is that you could win the biggest jackpot lottery on record, lay claim to the biggest gold mine in the world, strike it rich with your investments, become the heir to a family fortune, and still find yourself alone and friendless. The next time your friends gather at your table, look at each face and realize that each one is far more valuable than the crown jewels. Sharing their lives with you is a gift of unspeakable value. Whether you have one friend or twenty, treasure them. Do whatever you must to nurture and care for your friends. They are more precious than gold.

A Loving Wish for a Happy Day

A wish that's sent with lots of love
Just seems to have a feeling,
A special word of sentiment
That makes it more appealing.
And that's the kind of loving wish
That's being sent your way
To hope that every day will be
Your happy kind of day.

~ *HSR*

BY ALL MEANS POSSIBLE

Gracious speech is like clover honey—good taste to the soul, quick energy for the body.
PROVERBS 16:24 MSG

*A*mazing advances in technology have made letter writing all but a lost art. Snail mail is used these days primarily for bills, advertisements, and items that can't be easily delivered electronically. But that's exactly why getting a greeting by mail seems so special. It might be a humorous card to brighten the day of a friend who has been going though a tough time. Maybe it's just to say it has been too long since you got together. There are so many reasons not only to speak words of kindness and hope but also to write them down. It's a good idea to have cards on hand, but if you don't, remember it's the message rather than the package. Gracious words, loving words, encouraging words will decorate any plain old piece of paper.

This is a wonderful way to convey your love and devotion to a friend, but certainly not the only way. Take advantage of your e-mail, instant messaging, text messaging, even social networks to let your friends know how much they mean to you.

The Bible is filled with God's words of life and encouragement to us—His friends. It is in fact a letter to us from Him. He loves us so much that He went to the trouble of putting His thoughts into words so we would always know how He feels.

By all means possible, let your friends know how grateful you are that they are in your life.

STRANGERS ARE FRIENDS WE HAVEN'T MET YET

God knows no strangers; He loves us all:
The poor, the rich, the great, the small.
He is a Friend who is always there
To share our troubles and lessen our care.
For no one is a stranger in God's sight,
For God is love, and in His light
May we, too, try in our small way
To make new friends from day to day.
So pass no stranger with an unseeing eye,
For God may be sending a new friend by.

~HSR

STRANGERS AND FRIENDS

Contribute to the needs of the saints; extend hospitality to strangers.
ROMANS 12:13 NRSV

When we love someone very much, we often can't imagine our lives before that person was part of it. That's the way it is with spouses and children, of course, but it's also the way we feel about our true friends. We wonder what we did with our time before they came along. Wouldn't it have been a tragedy if two people, the best of friends, had failed to meet at all? If they had walked right past each other without saying a word or offering a welcoming gesture? They would have missed so much—blessings, fellowship, laughter, comfort, and shared affection. That's all the more reason for us to be diligent. We never know what wonderful relationships God has prepared for us.

Make sure you really look at the people you encounter every day. When it seems appropriate to do so, make eye contact and offer a word of greeting to those you already know and especially to those you do not. Even something as simple as a smile can be the beginning of a treasured friendship.

We humans tend to be creatures of habit. We feel safe with those we know. It takes courage to reach out to a complete stranger, to be the first to speak. We fear rejection. God risked rejection when He reached out to us, but it did not keep Him from doing all He could to let us know we are welcome in His presence.

HAPPINESS

*A*cross the years, we've met in dreams
And shared each other's hopes and schemes.
We've known a friendship rich and rare
And beautiful beyond compare. . .
But you reached out your arms for more
To catch what you were yearning for,
But little did you think or guess
That one can't capture happiness
Because it's unrestrained and free,
Unfettered by reality.

~*HSR*

Joy and Happiness

These things have I spoken unto you, that my joy might
remain in you, and that your joy might be full.
John 15:11 KJV

The Bible has quite a lot to say about the word *joy*. The word *happiness* is mentioned only a few times. It would seem that the two words are not synonymous, at least not in biblical terms. So what difference could there be?

Happiness is a temporary condition related to our external circumstances. Joy, on the other hand, transcends circumstance and is a state of mind—an attitude, a constant. It is based on the satisfaction and contentment we feel inside. It could be said that joy, unlike happiness, is a response to those things that have true worth or eternal value. We can lose our possessions and our status, but there are some things that cannot be taken away from us.

It would not be fair to say that we can't lose our friends. They come and go freely in our lives, and we are ultimately separated from some of them by death. However, those things we have invested in our friends—and they in us—cannot be lost. They are ours for good, and that brings joy to our hearts. When you place your trust, your love, your kindness, and your friendship in the hands of another person, that investment becomes an eternal commodity. And when that person chooses to reciprocate, the same is true.

We live in a time when so few things are certain. We do not know what will happen tomorrow. But we can always know that true friendship is an investment that will bring eternal joy.

JUST FRIENDS

Like ships upon the sea of life
We meet with friends so dear,
Then sail on swiftly from the ones
We'd like to linger near;
Sometimes I wish
The winds would cease,
The waves be quiet, too,
And let me sort of drift along
Beside a friend like you.

~HSR

Best Friends

"This is My commandment, that you love one another as I have loved you."
JOHN 15:12 NKJV

If you've ever had a "best" friend, you are well aware of how special that relationship can be. You count on each other. You challenge each other. You share things you would never share with anyone else on earth. It's like you each own a little of the other person's heart. And the best part? This relationship is almost effortless. When you're together there is no tension, no showing off, no pretense. You both just rest in each other's presence in a magical way.

This level of friendship is very dear and quite rare. It is a blessed relationship because it mirrors the relationship God wants to have with His friends—you and me. In this bond, there is a feeling of complete safety and trust. It makes you want to be a better person so that you can be a better friend. It includes mutual respect and deep, deep love.

Some people marry their best friend and build a life together. Others are separated by distance and time, but their bonds are never broken. When they see each other, regardless of how much time has passed, they pick up right where they left off.

God wants to be your best friend. Once you get to know Him, you will see that He is the perfect friend—steadfast and true!

Friendship Is Memories

Memory Rendezvous

*M*emory builds a little pathway that goes
     winding through my heart.
It's a lovely, quiet, gentle trail from other things apart.
I only meet when traveling there the folks I like the best,
For this road I call remembrance is hidden from the rest.
But I hope I'll always find you in my memory rendezvous,
For I keep this little secret place to meet with folks like you.

~HSR

ALSO KNOWN AS. . .

He who covers over an offense promotes love.
PROVERBS 17:9

*W*ithout the ability to remember, we would be like kites with broken strings, floating aimlessly from one breeze to the next. Our memories help us attach our past to our present, and together they form the beginnings of our future. And we have the amazing ability to choose what we remember and what we do not. In a sense, God has given us the ability to sort through our past, keep those things that are precious to us, and push the rest out of the way.

So what memories do you cherish? For most people, friends rank near the top of the "precious" list. It isn't unusual for people to remember their first childhood friend or friends who touched their lives for just a brief time. When friends get together, they often recall the things they did together in the past—their common memories.

Perhaps there is someone in your life, a former friend, who still lingers in your memory. It could be that this friend did something that pulled the two of you apart. You should know that you have the power to restore that friendship, if you choose. Use your God-given ability to keep the good memories and push the bad ones out of the way. Interestingly, this process has an alias—it's also known as forgiveness.

DISCOURAGEMENT AND DREAMS

So many things in the line of duty
Drain us of effort and leave us no beauty,
And the dust of the soul grows thick and unswept,
The spirit is drenched in tears unwept.
But just as we fall beside the road,
Discouraged with life and bowed down with our load,
We lift our eyes, and what seemed a dead end
Is the street of dreams where we meet a friend.

~ *JSR*

IN TIME OF NEED

Two are better than one, because they have a good return for their work:
If one falls down, his friend can help him up.
ECCLESIASTES 4:9–10

Think about your closest friends for a moment. Then take a little inventory. How many of them did you bond with during a time of hardship or difficulty? You might be surprised by the answer. For some reason, friendships seem to flourish during hard times, probably just because we are more in need of a reassuring face.

Perhaps you have a friend who saw you through a time of illness, holding your hand while you listened to the test results, helping to cover your responsibilities at work, listening while you talked through your fears and anxieties. Of course, your time of trial might not have been illness. It might have been financial hardship, the loss of a loved one, a divorce, or another of life's calamities. The principle is the same. Someone stood beside you and helped you through a dark valley in your life. Now your memories of that painful time are mitigated by the love and faithfulness of that special, loving friend.

Those friends who were there when it mattered—the ones who cried with us when our dream was crushed, the ones who assured us our dream would rise from the ashes—they are among God's greatest kindnesses. He is always there for us, but in His wisdom He knows we sometimes need the comfort of another human heart. Take time to remember those special friends and thank God for sending them your way.

TENDER LITTLE MEMORIES

*T*ender little memories
Of some word or deed
Give us strength and courage
When we are in need.
Blessed little memories
Help us bear the cross
And soften all the bitterness
Of failure and of loss.
Precious little memories
Of little things we've done
Make the very darkest day
A bright and happy one.

~HSR

THE LITTLE THINGS

He that is faithful in that which is least is faithful also in much.
LUKE 16:10 KJV

*I*f you are in the mood for a blessing (when wouldn't you be?), you might try this simple exercise. Find a quiet place, close your eyes, and remember. Take time to recall some of the wonderful times you've had with friends. Focus for a moment or two on each one. What special thing did that person bring to your life? What was the best time the two of you had together? Make a mental list of the specific acts of friendship you recall. Ask yourself what you can do to let that person know how much he or she means to you. Then thank God for sending that person your way.

This exercise is guaranteed to bring a smile to your face and bless your heart to overflowing. And in the process, you might realize a very important aspect of friendship. Most people remember the small things, the small kindnesses. These people may not have done anything to solve any specific problem you were having or rescue you from some situation you were in. Instead, they let you know in a hundred little ways that you were not alone. It is in these memories that you come to appreciate the comfort of a genuine hug, the soft voice that speaks words of hope and renewal, the simple gesture of an errand run or a meal cooked. True friendship isn't sustained by a single grand act, but rather by the little things that pass between friends day by day, year by year. Close your eyes again and reflect on the wonder of that.

ANOTHER LINK OF LOVE

*I*t takes a special day like this
To just look back and reminisce
And think of things you've shared together
Through sunny, fair, and stormy weather,
And how both smiles as well as tears
Endear true love across the years. . .
For there is no explaining of
The mystery of the bond of love,
Which just grows richer, deeper, stronger,
Because you've shared it one year longer.

~ *HSR*

Opposites Attract

As you think back over the years and reminisce about those friends you have loved so deeply and had so many wonderful times with, you may discover something odd. You may find yourself asking how you ever connected with certain friends who are so different from yourself. You might even find that some of these people are polar opposites of you in personality, temperament, and worldview. They may have vastly differing passions, dreams, strengths, and weaknesses.

This is more common than you might think. In fact, it is human nature to be drawn to those who exhibit characteristics you feel you don't have. This actually demonstrates one of the most blessed aspects of friendship—we tend to choose those who bring balance to our lives. You may be driven and ambitious, while your friend is laid back and content. You may be a dreamer, while your friend is a down-to-earth pragmatist. You may be a planner, while your friend relishes spontaneity. When you think about it, what would be the point of having friends who are just like you?

As you drift back through your memories, you are bound to remember a time when you avoided a mistake because a friend urged caution, or you took a chance that paid off because a friend urged you to go for your dream. Cherish those memories and revel in your differences. They are the spice of life!

Friendship Is Thankfulness

My Thanks

People everywhere in life, from every walk and station,
From every town and city and every state and nation,
Have given me so many things intangible and dear
I couldn't begin to count them all or even make them clear.
I only know I owe so much to people everywhere,
And when I put my thoughts in verse, it's just a way to share
The musings of a thankful heart, a heart much like your own,
For nothing that I think or write is mine and mine alone. . .
So if you found some beauty in any word or line,
It's just your soul's reflection in proximity with mine.

~HSR

DIFFERENT GIFTS

Each one should use whatever gift he has received to serve others,
faithfully administering God's grace in its various forms.
1 PETER 4:10

As you recall the special kindnesses your friends have brought to your life, you may wonder how you can thank them for all they've done for you. This can be simultaneously humbling and overwhelming.

How do you thank that friend who kept your children for a week while you recovered from surgery or that friend who pitched in and helped you finish a big work project on time, never asking for a bit of credit? How do you thank the friend who always remembers your birthday or the one who knows how to give you a good, solid smack-to-the-face pep talk?

Our friendships would be diminished if we were expected to reciprocate in kind. First of all, good friends do things for us because it's in their hearts to do them. They don't expect reciprocation. Second, we often cannot do for that friend what he or she has done for us. We have different gifts. You may not be capable of greeting each birthday with a card and a meticulously wrapped gift. You may not even be capable of remembering birthdays. But you can certainly bless a friend with an unexpected invitation to lunch. You may not be in a position to help a friend with a big project at work, but you can be there to listen to his ideas and offer encouragement.

Thank God for those special things your friends bring to your life, and show them how grateful you are by bringing your own special magic to theirs.

A Thankful Heart

*T*ake nothing for granted, for whenever you do,
The joy of enjoying is lessened for you.
For we rob our own lives much more than we know
When we fail to respond or in any way show
Our thanks for the blessings that daily are ours—
The warmth of the sun, the fragrance of flowers,
The beauty of twilight, the freshness of dawn,
The coolness of dew on a green velvet lawn,
The kind little deeds so thoughtfully done,
The favors of friends, and the love that someone
Unselfishly gives us in a myriad of ways,
Expecting no payment and no words of praise.
Oh, great is our loss when we no longer find
A thankful response to things of this kind.
For the joy of enjoying and the fullness of living
Are found in the heart that is filled with thanksgiving.

~HSR

Saying Thanks

We always thank God for all of you, mentioning you in our prayers. We continually remember before our God and Father your work produced by faith, your labor prompted by love, and your endurance inspired by hope in our Lord Jesus Christ.
1 Thessalonians 1:2–3

The one great flaw of close friendships is that we often take them for granted. When someone has always been there for us, we tend to expect that they always will be. This is just human nature. We should, though, on a regular basis take a few moments to remember and take note of the love shown to us by our true friends.

Thank-you notes are rare these days. We might send them when someone does us a huge favor or invites us to a party. But in truth, we tend to send them to acquaintances more often than friends. Somehow we get complacent about expressing our thankfulness to those who love us most. What a wonderful thing it would be to let each one know just how much their friendship means to you.

These expressions can come in many forms—a note on beautiful stationery, a standard thank-you card, or a greeting card (serious or funny). If you and your friends are more of the "tech set," a simple e-mail note might be most endearing. Post something on a social network for all to see. But whatever you do, take some time to thank those friends who make your life more beautiful, those who inspire, encourage, enlighten, and challenge you. Let them know you remember all the little things they've done for you by including a few of your favorite memories. This is sure to put a smile on each one of their faces.

Thank You, God, for Everything

Thank You, God, for everything—
   the big things and the small—
For every good gift comes from God, the Giver of them all,
And all too often we accept without any thanks or praise
The gifts God sends as blessings each day in many ways.
And so at this time we offer up a prayer
To thank You, God, for giving us a lot more than our share.
First, thank You for the little things that often come our way—
The things we take for granted and don't mention when we pray—
The unexpected courtesy, the thoughtful, kindly deed,
A hand reached out to help us in the time of sudden need.
Oh, make us more aware, dear God, of little daily graces
That come to us with sweet surprise from never-dreamed-of places.
Then thank You for the miracles we are much too blind to see,
And give us new awareness of our many gifts from Thee.
And help us to remember that the key to life and living
Is to make each prayer a prayer of thanks
   and each day a day of thanksgiving.

~HSR

The Gift of Friendship

*Every good and perfect gift is from above, coming down from the Father
of the heavenly lights, who does not change like shifting shadows.*

JAMES 1:17

God is so good to us! He showers us with blessings and holds
before us the promise of even more blessings in the life to
come. We should fill our hours and our days thanking Him
for all He has given us. He created and maintains the universe
so that we might be blessed by the earth beneath our feet, the
sunshine, and the rain. He moves the nations as He sees fit, in
order to carry out His purposes for us. He does so many things
on a grand stage, earning our praise and our awe. But He is not
just God of the big things. He also brings small and wonder-
ful blessings to our lives—and one of the greatest of those is
friendship.

Friends don't just happen to us; they are given to us. Our
paths don't just cross by accident; each one is orchestrated by
our heavenly Father. Like any earthly father, He wants to give
us good things, and so many good things come to us through
friendship.

God is pleased when we enjoy our friends, but as usual, He
has multiple purposes in mind. He knows that our friends keep
us steady in times of temptation, strong in times of trouble, and
sound in our thoughts and beliefs. They bring us perspective
and encouragement. They help God guard our hearts. We have
so much to be thankful for. Give God your thanks and praise
for the gift of friendship.

GIVE US DAILY AWARENESS

On life's busy thoroughfares
We meet with angels unawares.
So, Father, make us kind and wise
So we may always recognize
The blessings that are ours to take,
The friendships that are ours to make
If we but open our heart's door wide
To let the sunshine of love inside.
For God is not in far distant places
But in loving hearts and friendly faces.

~HSR

ZACCHAEUS'S HOUSE

When Jesus came by, he looked up at Zacchaeus and called him by name.
"Zacchaeus!" he said. "Quick, come down! I must be a guest in your home today."
LUKE 19:5 NLT

In order to make a friend, someone has to be willing to step up and initiate the relationship. Someone has to offer a kind word or extend a hand and a smile. Unless someone does, friends remain undiscovered and blessings go unclaimed.

In the Bible, there is a story about a man named Zacchaeus. He was eager to see Jesus, the teacher he had heard so much about. But the crowd was pressing, and he was a man of small stature. So Zacchaeus climbed a tree to get a better look. He must have been astonished when Jesus stopped at the base of the tree and spoke to him. Jesus called him by name and invited himself to dinner at Zacchaeus's house. This man was a tax collector, and an unpopular one at that, but Jesus extended His hand to him in friendship. By the time their evening together was over, Zacchaeus was a changed man.

Someone out there needs your friendship. It could be that person has been watching you from afar but has been unable to come any closer. Jesus was aware of Zacchaeus because He was listening to His Father's voice. Ask God who needs your outstretched hand of friendship. The person He points out to you may not be the most popular or charming person, but responding to God's voice and reaching out could change that person's life forever and give you a blessing you will always be thankful for.

A Friend Is a Gift from God

*A*mong the great and glorious gifts our heavenly Father sends
Is the gift of understanding that we find in loving friends. . .
For in this world of trouble that is filled with anxious care,
Everybody needs a friend with whom they're free to share
The little secret heartaches that lay heavy on the mind—
Not just a mere acquaintance, but someone who's just our kind. . .
For somehow in the generous hearts of loving, faithful friends,
The good God in His charity and wisdom always sends
A sense of understanding and the power of perception
And mixes these fine qualities with kindness and affection. . .
So when we need some sympathy or a friendly hand to touch
Or one who listens tenderly and speaks words that mean so much,
We seek a true and trusted friend
    in the knowledge that we'll find
A heart that's sympathetic and an understanding mind. . .
And often just without a word there seems to be a union
Of thoughts and kindred feelings,
    for God gives true friends communion.

~*HSR*

Popularity Is Overrated

Do not let loyalty and faithfulness forsake you;
bind them around your neck, write them on the tablet of your heart.
PROVERBS 3:3 NRSV

*Y*ou may be one of those people who has many friends around you all the time—so many that you hardly have enough time to spend with all of them. But then again, maybe you are the kind of person who struggles to find even one or two friends. No matter which one of these profiles fits you, it's interesting to note that as people grow older, they are more likely to say that they have found God's blessing in the quality of their friendships more so than in the number of them. Older individuals also tend to say they are somewhat surprised by which friends end up being the truest and most enduring.

Some friends only stick around for certain seasons of our lives, and there's nothing wrong with that. But some other friends are bonded to our hearts. They might not be the ones who most interest us at the beginning. They may not be bright and flashy and always in the forefront. But they are constant. We come to depend on them. They stay around even when it isn't very comfortable—when the music stops and we face grief, loss, and disappointment. They are faithful, loving, and stead-fast. These friends are God's gifts, pure and simple.

If you have one such friend, one person who will always be there for you, always forgive you, and always love you, be truly thankful. Popularity is overrated, really, but a tried and true friend? Now there's someone to cherish!

Life Is a Garden

Life is a garden, good friends are the flowers,
And times spent together are life's happiest hours. . .
And friendship, like flowers, blooms ever more fair
When carefully tended by dear friends who care. . .
And life's lovely garden would be sweeter by far
If all who passed through it were as nice as you are.

~ HSR

Roses, Tulips, Lilies, and Irises

Behold, how good and how pleasant it is for brethren to dwell together in unity!
PSALM 133:1 KJV

Our friends truly are flowers in the gardens of our lives—
for which we are ever grateful. And we have even more to be
thankful for when we realize that friendship doesn't have to be
a two-way street; it can also be a four-lane highway or a six-
lane expressway. A strong group of forever-friends can be one
of the greatest joys of life.

Human nature, to which we are all subject to some degree,
tends to be selfish and territorial. That's why friendship often
doesn't work in a group. But as believers, we have been given a
higher nature—the nature of Christ. When a group of friends
all love Christ and recognize Him as the center of their bond,
all things become possible. Each member, secure in God's love,
is free to enjoy the friendship of each of the others.

There are other advantages to group friendships as well. Such
groups can provide more color and more security than traditional
one-on-one friendships. Plus, there really is safety in numbers.
Jesus had twelve close friends. They walked side by side with
Him through the countryside and ministered to the people as a
group. They prayed together and talked through troubling
situations together. After Jesus' death, they formed the core
of the early church.

One long-stem rose is a beautiful sight. Two together will
take your breath away. But place those roses in a vase with tu-
lips, lilies, and irises. Well. . .we can only imagine!

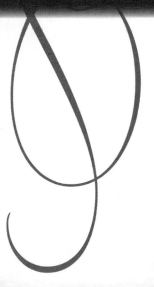

The Greatest Friend of All

God Is No Stranger

God is no stranger in a faraway place;
He's as close as the wind that blows 'cross my face.
It's true I can't see the wind as it blows,
But I feel it around me and my heart surely knows
That God's mighty hand can be felt everywhere,
For there's nothing on earth that is not in God's care.
The sky and the stars, the waves and the sea,
The dew on the grass, the leaves on a tree
Are constant reminders of God and His nearness,
Proclaiming His presence with crystal-like clearness.
So how could I think God was far, far away
When I feel Him beside me every hour of the day?
And I've plenty of reasons to know God's my friend,
And this is one friendship that time cannot end.

~ HSR

FRIENDSHIP WITH GOD

"No one has greater love than this, to lay down one's life for one's friends."
JOHN 15:13 NRSV

It's difficult to imagine, isn't it? The very God who created the universe, flinging billions of stars into the vast corners of space, wants to be friends with us. It's an absolutely mind-boggling concept—but apparently it's true! God hasn't left us to guess about it; He put it right there in the Bible.

For reasons known only to Him, God created us and this hospitable, warm earth we live on. Perhaps friendship is what He had in mind all along because He walked and talked with Adam and Eve in the lovely garden where they lived. But their times of fellowship ended when the garden dwellers betrayed Him. At that point, God could have just wiped His hands of the relationship and moved on. But instead, He went to extraordinary lengths to restore what they once had.

Our ideas about what friendship should be pale in comparison to God's. We learn from the Bible that He asked His only Son, Jesus, to leave the glory above and become one of us for two purposes: He needed someone to reintroduce us, and He needed someone worthy to heal the wound our betrayal left behind. He did all that and yet He never orders us to be His friends; He continues to ask.

God wants to be your friend. He has already made that opportunity possible. But He knows friendship cannot be mandated; both parties must be free to choose. Will you open your heart to Him?

My God Is No Stranger

I've never seen God, but I know how I feel.
It's people like you who make Him so real.
My God is no stranger—He's so friendly each day,
And He doesn't ask me to weep when I pray.
It seems that I pass Him so often each day
In the faces of people I meet on my way.
He's the stars in the heavens, a smile on some face,
A leaf on a tree, or a rose in a vase.
He's winter and autumn and summer and spring.
In short, God is every real, wonderful thing.
I think I might meet Him much more than I do
I would if there were more people like you.

~*HSR*

FACE-TO-FACE

"I have called you friends."
JOHN 15:15 NKJV

*F*riendship is God's invention—part and parcel of His creative genius. In this one wonderful package, He has included luscious servings of love, kindness, security, encouragement, enlightenment, challenge, joy, wisdom, and so much more. He urges us to have a circle of friends and then tells us He wants to be right in the center of that circle.

God not only invented friendship; He also teaches us what friendship is all about. Good friends are always there for each other, and God is always there for us. He says He will never leave us, never forsake us in good times or bad. Good friends tell us the truth, and God never clouds the truth. He lets us know when we are headed for trouble and going down the wrong path. Then He helps us get back to the safety of the main road. Good friends bring out the best in us, and God is always placing opportunities before us that will draw out the gifts He has placed in our lives. He wants each of us to fulfill the purpose for which we were born. Like all good friends, God gives us reason to be joyful in His presence, to trust Him without hesitation, and to rest safely in His love. He is a true friend!

One day we will see Him face-to-face, and then the friendship celebration will really begin. Until then, He shows us through the smiles, tender embraces, words of encouragement, and steadfastness of our friends here on earth.

Widen My Vision

God, open my eyes so I may see
And feel Your presence close to me.
Give me strength for my stumbling feet
As I battle the crowd on life's busy street,
And widen the vision of my unseeing eyes
So in passing faces I'll recognize
Not just a stranger, unloved and unknown,
But a friend with a heart that is much like my own.
Give me perception to make me aware
That scattered profusely on life's thoroughfare
Are the best gifts of God that we daily pass by
As we look at the world with an unseeing eye.

~HSR

A Friendship Prayer

Dear heavenly Father, what an honor it is to be called Your friend. It is the most remarkable privilege I can imagine. Help me to be a true friend to those You have placed in my life and to all those who need to feel Your hand of kindness and compassion. Amen.